# The Global Economic System

## Richard Lewis



ISBN: 9798880082834

# CONTENTS

# 1 INTRODUCTION

The origins of this book 4 lie way back in the 1970s at the height of the Cold War. I was working in the telecommunications industry in Canada and the company was working on the first data communication networks.

We realised that these data networks could be used for all sorts of communication that would change our lives. Organising the sale of products and services could be done through a centralised planned economy as with communism but with data networks in place an online market economy would be more efficient.

It was a heady time, the USA had just put men on the moon so everything was possible. We looked forward to the time when everyone had so much leisure time because of the efficiency gained from our wonderful technology. Food and clothing production would be automated, cars manufactured by robots and life would be wonderful.

But it didn't quite happen like that. The competitive work pressure increased. Government focused on maximising Gross Domestic Product over the interests of the people. More holidays would make us uncompetitive internationally.

Then the rise of China as a manufacturing location grew and imports destroyed local manufacturing. We encouraged it. We were getting good products at cheap prices but with a growing trade imbalance. We were living beyond our own means and going into debt.

Then you realise that the whole economic system is based on debt. When you buy a house, you get a mortgage and pay off the debt over a long period. The government started selling off national assets such as telephone, gas, electricity, water and rail. More efficient but the cost to the user went up and there were lots of new companies for the stock market and pensions. Not such a bad thing and I wouldn't suggest reversing this.

Then PFI contracts allowed government spending today based on repayment in the future. Student loans had a similar effect of transferring the debt to people so everyone got used to carrying some of the debt burden. We do seem to have created wealth but we as a country do seem to be consuming goods and services beyond the level of our work.

When we import goods from China they are paid for in UK pounds but they were manufactured using labour paid in Yuan. So China acquires a quantity of pound sterling. Presumably, they could sell these on the foreign exchange market for Yuan and the Bank of England would print a bit more money to cover for these imports. The UK manufacturing industry that previously manufactured these goods has gone but are we in greater debt as a country from this trade imbalance?

Of more concern is government debt. After all the efforts to balance the budget and do everything we need to do there is never enough and there is a worry that the piles and piles of international debt from government debt and trade imbalance will one day crash the global economy. It is hard to see a remedy which will move all countries to a positive bank balance. This could and probably should take 200 years to sort out.

Then you realise the money is just data in a computer transferred over data networks. We could just set up a central bank account and put money in it without going into debt. This would have to be through international agreement as described in the next chapter.

The purpose of our economic system is to allow the free trading of goods and services and to give people maximum freedom in their lives to live and work to their own goals. Just printing money will make our currency fall on foreign exchange markets.

But what if all countries created money in this way in proportion to their population? Then the currency levels could be preserved while reducing debt. Then perhaps we could use this new system as an incentive towards world peace.

The next chapter describes the proposed enhanced global economic system

One final introductory note on cryptocurrency. Cryptocurrency is a threat to financial stability. It is used by drug dealers, people traffickers, and other criminals. Rather than make it illegal we should tax each cryptocurrency transaction with a transaction charge. This should be effective in reducing the value of the cryptocurrency to close to zero and thus removing the potential harm.

# 2 THE GLOBAL ECONOMIC SYSTEM

For most of the 20th century on Earth there was an ideological battle between capitalism and communism. Capitalism was founded on a limited number of people having ownership of land, property and money and using it to good effect.

Communism was founded on the idea that the economy can be better managed centrally with common ownership and centrally managed five year plans.

Neither system in its extreme form was ideal and the centrally managed system proved to be far less economically effective when compared with a market economy.

It may have escaped our notice that the conflict between economic models has been replaced by an economic system which is very effectively managed by the use of computers and communication networks.

So we already have an economic system and this is operated by all participants with involvement of United Nations agencies, national governments, banks, central banks, stock exchanges, companies and individuals.

We have discovered some tools such as quantitative easing and interest rate management to help to ensure stability of currencies and optimum employment levels. The world economy is also affected by limits to growth and the effect of an increasing population.

The global economic system is intended as a description of our current system of economic management. This is characterised by the collective effect of all the nationally managed economic systems.

What we are looking for is an enhanced global economic system in which each nationally managed economic system benefits from the enhanced global economic system without political interference from other national governments.

The suggestion is to consider carefully what objectives we have for our global economic system. What are the objectives for global activity? Can we use the global economic system to fulfil world class goals to ensure the survival of the human race and other species?

**Enhanced Global Economic System**

There is the possibility of enhancing the global economic system to ease deprivation and provide a more optimum level of effective employment. Suppose we had a source of funding to help the economies of all countries individually.

We would create new money which would be administered by a new organisation called the Universal Bank. The Universal Bank would allocate funds to each country to the value of one dollar per person per day. The Universal Bank would work with the central banks in every country to manage the allocation of this new money to the national government. This would be new money created by global agreement.

For a country with a population of one hundred million the initial amount would be 36.5 billion dollars per year. For developed economies this would contribute to the national budget and could even be used to make payments towards reducing the national debt.

For developing economies, one dollar per person per day additional national spending is significant and could be used to improve education and healthcare or whatever is the national priority determined by the government of that country. Crucially this money would be allocated without the country incurring any debt burden.

There would be an experimental period of five years to see if there are unintended consequences for the enhanced global economic system. There would be an auditing process to ensure that there is no inappropriate use of the funds in each country. National governments have the objective of acting in the best interests of their own people and every country would benefit.

At the end of the five year period, if the enhanced global economic system is a success the funding level could be increased to two dollars per person per day with further increases later as long as the constraints are respected.

The ability to create money from nothing seems too good to be true. However, given that money is data stored within computers and transmitted by data networks, it is entirely feasible. Care must be taken to ensure that price inflation is kept under control but in some economies deflation has been a greater problem.

Only one bank, the universal bank would be authorised to provide funding to national governments without them incurring debt. The enhanced global economic system does carry some risks if the constraints listed below are not respected but it does represent an important opportunity to promote responsible global growth and ease deprivation.

## Constraints

The enhanced global economic system has the potential to lead to price inflation and has to be managed accordingly. We must use this method of creating new money in a responsible way to manage inflation while optimising global activity. The key point with this form of funding is that we can create new money without creating new indebtedness.

There are limits to growth which have to be respected. Population growth is often reduced in the more developed economies which suggests that population growth will reduce in developing countries as they develop economically. The availability of natural resources and the protection of the environment have to be considered as constraints on global development. The environment is a key constraint but also an opportunity for funding to promote clean air and oceans and manage waste products arising from human activity.

Mass migration of people from one country to another has the effect of destabilising the host country and is not in the best interests of the host country or the migrants themselves. The Enhanced Global Economic

System has to be aimed at solving the problems in each country that make people want to leave. Only once we have recovered from past wars and stabilised the situation will there be the opportunity to open up migration which is likely to take place in both directions between the developed and the developing world.

The development of the enhanced global economic system depends on national governments acting in a responsible way in the best interests of their own people and of the planet as a whole. Within these constraints we have in the enhanced global economic system the ability to create the financial resources by common agreement to implement development projects for the welfare of all the nations to meet their basic needs and more.

**Objectives**

An objective of the enhanced global economic system is to ease deprivation at the national and international level. Furthermore the enhanced global economic system has the potential to address global problems such as climate change, loss of diversity, and to create a sustainable future.

It is an important objective to stabilise the global population and this will be a natural result of human education and development. When the population of a country is no longer increasing this has a tendency to create a lack of economic growth leading to recession and deflation but this can be reversed by the funding derived from the enhanced global economic system.

One of the results of the COVID-19 pandemic has been to reduce economic activity and create unemployment. Governments are trying to resolve this by spending more, reducing interest rates and using quantitative easing. This approach can be supplemented by providing increased funding to national governments but without the increased national debt which arises from government borrowing.

As part of the global effort to ease deprivation extra funds provided by the enhanced global economic system could be used to rebuild countries ravaged by war and to help solve the refugee crisis affecting many countries.

Where there are high levels of unemployment, the use of funding from the enhanced global economic system could be used to increase economic activity. Where there is high unemployment we simply have to look at the problems that the government needs to address with increased spending.

National governments must not allow mass unemployment. It is a question of setting global and national priorities for what needs to be done. It is for national governments to set priorities for the use of the available resources in a fair and sustainable way.

There is so much that needs to be done. Spending in areas of scientific research, housing, infrastructure, physical and mental health, social care, eliminating scams and fraud, reducing the use of illegal drugs, addressing climate change and pollution and managing nuclear waste are all on the list of priorities.

This means that we must permanently shift the balance of the economy so that the public sector represents a substantially greater percentage of the Gross Domestic Product (GDP) than the private sector and with the contribution of the enhanced global economic system there will be no need for tax increases.

The funding from the enhanced global economic system allows the people of the country to have the financial benefit in goods and services without the country as a whole having to earn that money through international trade because all countries are benefitting in a fair and equal way. The drive for exports often causes unintended consequences such as the destruction of the rain forests.

It is important for the sake of fairness for the national funding to be based on population so we are in effect giving everyone in the world X dollars per person per day of free income even though the funding goes to the national government to spend in the best interests of their people and the future of the planet.

The process of setting the funding level has to be put in place under the control of the United Nations and this would take the form of a global monetary policy committee (GMPC). Given the experimental nature of the enhanced global economic system it would be prudent to put in place monitoring systems to observe the effect of the enhanced funding on each country and to monitor inflation within each country.

Finally, should there be pre-conditions on the allocation of funds from the enhanced global economic system to any particular country? Given that the funds are to be used in the best interests of the people, it would seem reasonable to require that the national government must be elected by the people, free of corruption and dedicated to the freedom and human rights of the individual.

Each country benefitting from the enhanced global economic system must have a written constitution with limitations on the term of office of any leader to a maximum of two terms of office and a maximum of ten years in office in total.

## Appendix 1 Control of Price Inflation

The role of the UK Monetary Policy Committee (MPC) is to control price inflation in the UK through the control of the bank interest rate. If inflation went up in the past the MPC would raise interest rates with the objective of reducing inflation. There is a strong argument that this is no longer an appropriate response.

In the past the idea was that by raising interest rates, it reduces the spending power of people with house mortgages and therefore the money in circulation is reduced and prices come down. This is a very tough way of controlling inflation and is likely to lead to a recession. It also unfairly penalises people with house mortgages. It is also likely in the current economic system that an increase in interest rates would cause more price inflation. Businesses that rely on borrowing to sustain their business model will see increased costs and will be forced to raise prices further.

In the future we will need to take a different approach to controlling price inflation. We will have to look in detail at the underlying cause of the price inflation. If it is in food products, is it because of changes in agricultural subsidy? If it is because of changes to currency exchange rates or tariffs perhaps the adjustment will come about by more local production. If the inflation is due to cost of raw materials such as the price of fossil fuels then perhaps the inflation in this area should be allowed in order to encourage a move away from fossil fuels. There is a balance to be struck and if the price of fuel is too inflationary then perhaps there is room to adjust vehicle fuel taxation downwards. VAT rates can also be used to manage price inflation.

Where there is free market competition, this should be sufficient to control price inflation at a level where businesses are able to make a profit. Price inflation will then arise if conditions change in such a way to make these businesses unprofitable. The ideal remedy then is to address the underlying cause that is affecting the profitability of the business. The remedy could include a change to business rates and corporate taxation.

The important point is that changes of taxation to manage inflation can be undertaken without governments being so concerned about the effect on government borrowing if the gap between government taxation and spending is filled to some extent by the enhanced global economic system.

There is an argument in favour of a controlled and planned increase in national interest rates by around 0.1% per annum starting at the year of launch of the enhanced global economic system to reach a level of 1% for the bank interest rate. This will give some income to savers and will move us away from a position where there is a possibility of negative interest rates which are to be avoided. [This paper was first printed when interest rates were close to zero (2020) ]

**Appendix 2 Using the banking system to combat crime**

The growing use of digital technology in financial transactions has meant that we are making less use of cash. This has also created opportunities for criminals to exploit the situation through scams and fraud.

This has a highly detrimental effect on society because it undermines trust. When you receive a phone call on your home telephone you expect it to be a scam.

So we have to deploy the banking system to combat all criminal activity which is motivated by profit. The proceeds of crime are the motivating factor for many categories of crime including drug trafficking and people trafficking as well as the cases of scams and fraud.

If it were possible to trace through the banking system and recover any money taken illegally then there would be no profit to the criminals. The banking systems might need to be adapted to give specific secure access to organised crime police departments with the immediate authority to freeze accounts. The administrative problems for the legal system in dealing with such crimes would be great but once it was seen to be effective and no money was to be made through this criminal activity, then the activity itself would diminish reducing the policing and legal costs.

It should be part of the supervisory responsibility of the central banks to make sure that the clearing banks take action with their banking systems to make the financial transactions traceable and recoverable. This has to be an international effort.

It should also be the collective responsibility of the central banks to make sure that all financial transactions are traceable and recoverable including all cryptocurrency.

Until this problem is sorted out, the central banks should not even consider introducing their own digital currency. At present the clearing banks are doing an amazing job in dealing with and refunding losses for some forms of scams and fraud.

There is a concern for the privacy of financial transactions and this is a legitimate concern. However, the breakdown of trust within society is a big problem and some relinquishment of privacy to properly authorised organisations is necessary to resolve the problem. If your financial transaction is legal you have no reason to require ultimate privacy from authorised criminal investigators. The financial transactions remain private in all other respects.

## Appendix 3 Nuclear Waste

The problem of nuclear waste is mentioned here because of the huge and growing liability which is being incurred. The cost of dealing with nuclear waste is being understated even in the latest proposals for nuclear power stations. It is the most toxic radioactive waste products which have lifetime of ten to one hundred thousand years which are of most concern. In the financial planning it is assumed that the most radioactive materials can be buried deep underground where they are inaccessible and only a one-off cost is incurred for that waste material.

This is irresponsible and the waste material has to be accessible and the ongoing cost of inspection and maintenance has to be included. When it is realised that this cost applies over the entire lifetime of the nuclear waste it becomes clear that nuclear power is not and never was economically viable.

All the nuclear power stations in the UK and in many other parts of the world are located near the coast where they are vulnerable to unforeseen events and catastrophic failures lead to ground contamination for decades.

The plan for the phased decommissioning of ageing nuclear power stations should include the storage facility for various grades of nuclear waste and a provision for the decommissioning of nuclear weapons.

The timescale for a storage and inspection facility for nuclear waste is probably measured in terms of hundreds of years. Whether nuclear weapons decommissioning takes place in a hundred years time or a thousand years time will depend on a secure level of trust between nations. We can be sure that whichever timescale it is for the removal of nuclear weapons, we will still be dealing with the problem of nuclear waste at that time.

Some provision will be needed from the enhanced global economic system to cover the ongoing costs of nuclear waste management.

# 3 PEACE PLAN

The global economic system provides an incentive for world peace and so it makes sense to make a plan which reflects this goal. The timescales seem very long but it takes time to adjust to a new cultural outlook and to build trust between nations.

## 2030 to 2050: End international conflict

The plan starts in 2030 under the assumption that it will take until 2030 to engage the attention of the countries of the world towards this objective. Then hopefully the period 2030 to 2050 will be a period when trust is building and the enhanced global economic system is developing to anchor the commitment to peace. Governments need to do their job in managing the national issues of their own country rather than getting involved in the domestic issues of other countries. The key element is to build trust between nations.

## 2050 to 2100: End geopolitics

We will not be able to end the divisive effect of geopolitics until international conflict is over. There is then no reason to seek military superiority even though national spending on defence is still needed. The objective is to put all countries on an equal footing so that there is no sense in which one nation is superior or with global International responsibilities. It will take time for the news media to let go of their role in reporting on conflicts around the world and speculating on who is the most powerful.

The news media do not help the situation with their focus on geopolitics. Freedom of the press is important and it will take time to effect cultural change to end geopolitics.

There are many people with a vested interest in warfare. Governments wanting to stay in power, the arms manufacturers, the news media, NATO. This is one of the greatest challenges in securing a lasting peace. Weapons production will have to continue long after peace is established just to maintain a defensive capability until we can really trust everyone.

## 2100 to 2150: Constitutional reform to end civil wars and limit individual power.

Constitutional reform can be led by the United Nations to define best practice. Country leaders  are selected by the people and a constraint on the term of office will limit the rise of dictators and tyrants. A constitution provides a means of avoiding civil war by providing a mechanism for devolution and independence of nations within a country if there is the need for such devolution. A referendum of the people is a good choice for such a decision but the constitutional arrangements for separation have to be stated in the constitution so everyone understands what will happen. With economic system funding by population count this will help the sustainability of smaller nations and there should be no defence alliances needed by this time.

Starting in each country when they are ready, the constitution is the means by which any evolution of the governance of the country is to be managed. The constitution can control the separation of church and state if required, the change from a constitutional monarchy to a constitutional presidency if appropriate and means of devolution of nations if this applies.

In the period up to 2100 it is hoped that international conflict can be avoided. Where there are devolution ambitions these will hopefully be postponed until 2100 given the knowledge that devolved nationhood is in the plan. As part of the constitutional process the structure of government limiting the power of individuals will be included in the constitution. The constitution can include an obligation to hold a referendum on nuclear weapons every 10 years.

## 2150 to 2200: Nuclear disarmament by referendum of the people

An extended period of peace and stability and trust will be needed for the people to vote in a referendum for unilateral nuclear disarmament. As long as there are nuclear weapons in the world no-one is free. This plan shows how nuclear weapons could be abolished by 2200. It is important not to rush the process because it takes many years for trust to build up between nations.

This approach gives national autonomy within an international framework of guiding principles from the United Nations with incentives built into the Global Economic System.

# 4 GROWTH VERSUS SUSTAINABILITY

**Growth versus sustainability (UK)**

We need an economic model based on sustainability. This is a move away from having the primary objective of GDP growth. The objective should be stable population numbers so that the level of immigration allowed compensates for the expected declining birth rate. The level of population migration can be managed by requiring that new people entering the country must have jobs before they arrive and with the salary above a specified threshold. If there are too many entering we would have to raise the salary threshold for future visa applications.

[Illegal migration across the channel is unsafe and has to be stopped. The Royal Navy will patrol the English channel with boats using observation drones. Once a migrant boat enters international waters it will be intercepted. The migrants attempting this dangerous crossing will be taken by landing craft back to the Normandy beaches. There they will be taken into custody by the French police for the illegal act of trying to cross the English Channel in an unsafe vessel. The inflatable boat will be impounded and destroyed.]

It is for the enhanced global economic system to resolve the problem of mass migration in the long term.

For each country, the objective will be to raise the standard of living and quality of life for everyone. Progressive increase in holiday entitlement from 28 days to 40 days over a 5 year period is designed to mitigate the pressure of modern living.

The new measure of success is the Percentage Cost of Basic Needs (PCBN). This measures the cost of basic needs as a percentage of income. PCBN is improved by wage increases and harmed by interest rate rises and inflation.

We should no longer try to use interest rates to control inflation. The Central Bank should use interest rates to maintain the value of the currency. The objective will be to get interest rates down to one percent but the change should follow gradually in line with the USA interest rate.

The government will be responsible for controlling inflation. This is largely caused by  international price changes although wage settlements in the UK can be inflationary too. Food prices can be subsidised to favour local production which is most necessary for sustainability of UK food supply. The precise subsidy model should be generous and encourage employment in the farming sector by paying 50% of the wage bill of farm workers. In other sectors prices are generally controlled by competition and the government has a responsibility to ensure competitive markets are operating effectively.

Low interest rates tend to lead to increased house prices which adversely affects PCBN. The purchase of UK property by non-residents is to be disallowed. This also applies to land and to foreign companies and foreign sovereign funds buying up assets in the UK.

To be sustainable we have to ensure that we meet our basic needs through our own efforts and not primarily through imports. We need an assessment of the national debt built up over the years through the trade balance and government borrowing. We also need to know the level of UK pounds held by foreign governments.

Unemployment may rise or fall but we need increased staffing and funding in the public sector in areas like healthcare and education, police and armed forces. The level of employment in the public sector compared with the private sector is expected to increase through salary increases in the public sector to restore living standards.

China is deliberately holding down the Yuan exchange rate to make their goods competitive internationally. We have benefitted from these low prices but wage rates in China will rise and the Yuan exchange rate will bring the wage rates in China more in line with the UK and USA. This will provide a competitive opportunity to regain some of the manufacturing jobs that have been lost. This would improve our balance of trade and provide useful local employment. The saving on transportation costs would be a competitive advantage and the reduced transportation helps with climate change.

We want people to have real family lives again and bring up the next generation with a goal of making the world a better place doing jobs without the stress that this generation has created unnecessarily.

## UK tax changes

There are a number of opportunities for changes to the UK tax system.

**Taxes to be cancelled**: council tax, business rates, inheritance tax.

Local government to be funded by central government at a level of £2,500 per household.

BBC licence fee to be paid by central government for all households.

## New taxes:

Flight tax at £250 per UK takeoff or landing. Northern Ireland exempt.

Petrol and diesel climate tax at 50p per litre

Tax on burning gas in electric power stations. Save gas for use in home boilers which need not be phased out. Then increase wind power generation. Home UPS facility controlled from the grid to store excess wind power for later use.

Tax on home and land ownership by non-UK citizens.

Tax on visiting students using UK education system.

Increase VAT to 25%

These tax changes are aimed at significantly improving the Percentage Cost of Basic Needs (PCBN) by removing council tax and BBC licence fee

# 5 NUCLEAR WASTE

The problem of nuclear waste has been covered in Chapter 2 and in this chapter an approach to solving the problem is proposed.

Storing High Level Nuclear Waste

Abstract

There is an unresolved problem in the nuclear industry of dealing with high level nuclear waste. This nuclear waste is in the form of spent fuel rods or surplus material from nuclear weapons or highly radioactive material from reprocessing. The problem is that the material stays radioactive in some cases for 10,000 or even 100,000 years and so any containment vessel cannot be guaranteed to remain effective for such a long period of time. This means that a regime of inspection and remedy is required. When a containment vessel fails we have to deal with the entire contaminated product which now consists of the waste material and the failed container. This proposal gives a strategy for dealing with this problem.

**Containment system**

The plan is to start with quantities of nuclear waste material which will fit inside a 20 cm cube. This gives eight litres of storage and any material placed in a container would need to be well below the critical mass for the type of waste. It would also be necessary to have a facility which prepares the nuclear waste on the site of the power station or nuclear research facility and divides it into smaller pieces which will fit inside the container. The interior dimension of the base container is 20 cm and the base container walls would be 19 cm thick giving an exterior dimension of 58 cm cube.

The target life for the base container (level 1) will be a minimum of 100 years with the objective that 99% of containers will remain intact for this period. The level 2 container would have an interior dimension of 60 cm and a wall thickness of 9 cm giving an external dimension of 78 cm. The level 3 container would have an interior dimension of 80 cm and a wall thickness of 9 cm giving an external dimension of 98cm. The level 4 container would have an interior dimension of 100 cm and a wall thickness of 9 cm giving an external dimension of 118 cm.

The level 1 container would be rated at 100 years. When placed inside a level 2 container the rating is increased to 1000 years. When placed inside a level 3 container the rating is increased to 10,000 years. When placed inside a level 4 container the rating is increased to 100,000 years.

Initially it is sufficient to have a good design for the level 1 container. Then we have approximately 100 years to design really effective level 2 container. Then we have 1000 years available to design a really effective level 3 container. The cost of the level 2, 3 and 4 container systems could well be very high using special materials and so they would only be used when the lower level container fails.

**Access system**

Each portion of nuclear waste is identified and allocated to a particular numbered level 1 container. The waste material would be prepared and placed in the level 1 container on the nuclear site and then this container would be placed inside a transport container for delivery to the waste storage facility.

The waste storage facility would make use of tunnelling technology currently available for high speed rail projects and the rail tunnels would be directly accessible from the surface. The waste storage facility would not be deep underground and should be located away from the coast in a geographically suitable location.

The trains operating within the storage facility would be fully automatic with no human intervention except for rail network servicing. The level 1 containers would be placed in concrete pods alongside the track and would be put in place by a robotic arm operated from the train. Each container of nuclear waste would have an allocated position which it will retain for its entire life.

**Servicing**

The principle of operation is that the containers are checked periodically and if radioactivity is detected at a particular level 1 container the entire level 1 container is placed inside a level 2 container and returned to the same position. This means that even though the level 1 container is only 58cm x 58 cm x 58 cm the place allocated for its storage beside the track allows for sufficient space for a level 4 container which has a base of 118cm x 118cm.

**Cost analysis**

This approach to storing and maintaining high level nuclear waste has to be costed based on the quantity of nuclear waste material to be stored. There will also be an ongoing operating cost for the rail system and the robotic trains.

The upfront construction cost for the system could be as high as a typical high speed rail project but this is a realistic cost for dealing with such an intractable problem. Once such a system has been costed it will be possible to specify a fixed cost and a variable cost associated with dealing with the high level nuclear waste. The variable cost will provide a figure for use in nuclear power projects to assess the unit cost of dealing with the spent fuel rods.

# 6 PROPOSED UK CONSTITUTION

We the people of England, Scotland, Wales and Northern Island who seek an elected government to establish justice, promote the general welfare of the people and secure the blessings of freedom and liberty for the people, do establish and ordain this constitution.

In placing authority in the hands of government, the people electing their leaders form a compact for good governance. The ultimate power rests with the people through elections and referenda. History shows that progress is best achieved through evolution and not revolution. Where revolutions take place it may subsequently result in power being taken away from the people for hundreds of years or more. In this case the people have no recourse to remove tyrants and autocratic regimes.

So the government of the United Kingdom must respond to the evolutionary will of the people and provide for democratic change rather than revolutionary change. In the United Kingdom power rests with the executive branch of government and not the crown. It follows that the constitutional monarchy rests in existence subject to the will of the people. Even though there may be no wish to evolve from a constitutional monarchy, this constitution makes it clear that the decision to move to a constitutional presidency rests with the people, the electorate of the United Kingdom.

An important principle established over the centuries is the separation of church and state. This brings with it the freedom of worship so that people may follow any religion that does not adversely impact on the common welfare. The secular head of state must relinquish their role as the defender of the faith and the head of the Church of England. All religions in the UK need to adapt to the scientific reality that there is no life after death and this would be a matter for the new governing body of the church of England to address.

Given the importance of good governance, much importance must also be attached to the process of election. With the growth of public media advertising and the ability to influence the result of elections, there must be limits on the type and magnitude of election expenditure. Election expenditure should be limited to that needed to put forward the policies or manifesto of the political party and the intentions of the constituency candidates were they to be elected. It should not be possible to buy the result of an election.

The system of political parties is called into question and the change to a parliament of independent MPs (freedom parliament) is proposed subject to a decision by parliament. The system of political parties has resulted in adversarial politics with politicians acting in the best interests of the political party rather than the best interests of the country. In a freedom parliament each constituency MP would be elected by their constituents as an independent. After the election of MPs by the electorate, the MPs would choose their prime minister and the cabinet. There would be no party organisations, no whips and all MPs would cooperate to arrive at the best decisions for the country. All MPs would be able to challenge government decisions in parliament.

It has long been the case that it is the news media that hold the government to account for its actions. To recognise this role, the BBC licence fee would no longer be paid by the people but by the government. The licence fee represents an unfair kind of poll tax. The BBC would retain its independence and would retain its status as a not for profit organisation. Any development of the legacy assets of the BBC for income would be a saving for the country. The BBC would continue in its excellent role of challenging the decisions and priorities of the government. Other media organisations would freely participate in this role. What would disappear in a freedom parliament is the stoking of the divisions between political parties by the news media for the entertainment of their audience.

The constitution of the United Kingdom which comprises England, Scotland, Wales and Northern Ireland must include provision for Scotland, Wales or Northern Ireland to leave the union if it is the will of the people in those individual nations. This constitution provides the basis for the orderly transition for Scotland, Wales and Northern Ireland to become independent countries.

The protection of human rights is encompassed within this constitution in such a way as to retain the sovereignty of the United Kingdom. A transition is to be made away from subjugation to the European convention on human rights which would involve cases in the United Kingdom being taken to the courts in a foreign country. The proposed solution is to construct and adopt a United Kingdom convention on human rights based heavily on the European convention but adjudicated by the courts in England, Scotland, Wales and Northern Ireland.

The founding principle of this constitution is the right of people to chose their own leaders and to ensure that the power of those leaders is constrained to avoid the rise of dictators and autocratic leaders who will extend their own term of office.

The constitutional arrangements complete the move away from the British empire. The British commonwealth is a relic of empire and is to be phased out. The UK Overseas Territories will be encouraged to become independent countries with their own constitution.

The objective is for every country around the world to be independent and free from interference by other countries.

The UK is to withdraw from all military alliances. History shows that the military alliances in place at the time of the first world war resulted in a fast escalation of the conflict. When the Warsaw Pact nations dissolved their military alliance, an opportunity was missed to respond by dissolving NATO. The existence of NATO has been a contributory factor in the war in Ukraine.

The UK should not be bound by a military alliance and have freedom of action to deploy military force when needed and following the agreement of parliament. The UK is then focussed on domestic issues and the defence spending is primarily for defence. However, if a UK overseas territory, newly independent, were attacked by another country then there would be strong justification of a military response from the UK in attacking the aggressor.

In the past there has been a tendency to use the UK parliament as a forum for geopolitical posturing on the affairs of other countries. The UK parliament should restrict its discussions to UK domestic matters. It is not helpful to take sides in a foreign civil war and many conflict situations would be resolved more quickly if other countries withdrew all military aid from the region and enabled the peace negotiation.

**Article 1: United Kingdom Legislative branch**

**Section 1: The House of Commons**

The members of parliament (MPs) elected to the house of commons have the responsibility for setting the law of the land through acts of parliament. The combined effect of all acts of parliament past and present represents the law of the land on the basis of which judgements are made in the courts of law of the judicial branch.

MPs represent the people of their constituency that elected them to the parliament and by taking on this role they must undertake to resign from any paid employment which they had prior to the election. To avoid any conflict of interest, MPs must not receive payment for any services outside their role as a member of the parliament.

## Section 2: The House of Lords

The house of lords reads and responds to legislation passed by the house of commons. After consideration, review and debate in the house of lords the proposed act of parliament may be amended before returning the legislation to the house of commons for further consideration.

The house of lords also provides judicial review of certain categories of action by the executive branch.

Members of the house of lords are appointed by the government and may continue as a  member of the house of lords for life or until they chose to retire. Members of the house of lords may have other employment outside of their parliamentary responsibilities but paid lobbying is not permitted and any potential conflict of interest must be declared.

## Section 3: The Head of State

The countries of England, Scotland, Wales and Northern Ireland together form a single country of four nations named the United Kingdom. The form of government is named a constitutional monarchy in which the head of state is a king or queen.

The responsibility of head of state passes from the current king or queen to their next descendent with the oldest male or female descendent having priority.

An act of parliament will pass into the statute books and become law if it is signed by the head of state. This constrains the ultimate power of the elected government and prevents the rise of autocratic leaders who wish to amend the constitution to extend their term of office.

Depending on the will of the people, the form of government in the United Kingdom can be changed from a constitutional monarchy to a constitutional presidency with an elected president. The decision to move to a constitutional presidency will be possible in a referendum of the people taken every ten years starting in 2050 and if such a decision is taken then the president takes on the role of head of state.

Traditionally the King or Queen engages with the people to project power and majesty. This role may continue but the other roles of the head of state are more important. The head of state must defend the constitution against the rise of tyrants or dictators. The head of state must have a receptive channel of communication with the citizens of the country who may wish to raise concerns about the actions of government. Such concerns would be prioritised by the head of state and advisors and discussed with the prime minister at the monthly meeting.

In a constitutional presidency, the role of president will be to act as head of state. Executive power still rests with the executive branch of government. The president is elected for a ten year term of office with the possibility of a second term if duly elected.

## Section 4: Legislative branch in England, Scotland, Wales and Northern Ireland

The law of the land differs in the nations of the United Kingdom and there are five categories:

1. Laws that apply throughout the United Kingdom. These are the laws of the United Kingdom

2. Laws that apply only in England. These are the laws of England.

3. Laws that apply only in Scotland. These are the laws of Scotland.

4. Laws that apply only in Wales. These are the laws of Wales

5. Laws that apply only in Northern Ireland. These are the laws of Northern Ireland.

Acts of the UK parliament have been passed which define the scope of legislation for the devolved government in Scotland, Wales and Northern Ireland. The law of the land as applied within each nation (England, Scotland, Wales and Northern Ireland) shall be the national law and the United Kingdom law combined.

## Article 2 United Kingdom Executive Branch

### Section 1: Executive power

The executive power shall be vested in the prime minister and the cabinet formed following the general election.

The prime minister shall hold office during the term of the parliament unless removed by a vote of no confidence in parliament. The maximum period of office of a prime minister is ten years not necessarily served in one term of office.

The prime minister will lead a cabinet of MPs who are chosen to take specific responsibilities such as finance, health care and defence.

## Section 2: Military deployment

The government comprising the prime minister and cabinet have responsibility for proposing the deployment of military forces. Any deployment of the United Kingdom military forces requires the approval of parliament.

Any supply of military equipment to other countries requires the approval of parliament.

## Section 3: Nuclear weapons

Nuclear weapons are held as a deterrent. For people to be truly free, all nuclear weapons around the world must be decommissioned. To have full nuclear disarmament it is necessary for a level of trust between the countries of the world to be reached so that each country feels that they can safely remove their nuclear weapons.

Starting in the year 2150, a referendum is to be held in the United Kingdom every ten years for the people to decide if they chose for the country to decommission and destroy their own nuclear weapons. This presupposes an end to international conflict by 2050 and an end to geopolitics by 2100. Then a decision on unilateral nuclear disarmament by the United Kingdom or England is likely to lead to a similar decision in turn by other nuclear powers if they have followed a similar political path towards peace.

## Section 4: Executive branch in England, Scotland, Wales and Northern Ireland

The executive branch of the United Kingdom directly holds executive power in England. The executive branch of the devolved government in the nations of Scotland, Wales and Northern Ireland holds power as defined by previous acts of parliament.

## Article 3: Judicial Branch

There is to be a separate judiciary for England, Scotland, Wales and Northern Ireland. The judiciary within the national boundary has responsibility for the legal system and law courts operating within that boundary. The appeal system allows appeals to the highest court which is the supreme court for that national territory. For example the supreme court of Scotland will hear cases which arise in Scotland and are brought under the laws of Scotland and the laws of the United Kingdom.

Cases in England will be brought to the English courts by the England prosecution service not the crown prosecution service. Similarly in Scotland, Wales and Northern Ireland cases will be brought to the national courts by the national prosecution service for that nation. The people of the United Kingdom are citizens of the United Kingdom not subjects of the crown.

The legislative branch is responsible for setting the laws as applied by the judicial branch in the law courts. There is to be strict separation between the legislative branch and the judicial branch. Neither the executive branch nor the legislative branch are involved in deciding the outcome of any particular legal case. The judicial branch is not responsible for setting the laws.

It is a basic human right to have a clear statement of the law when defending a case. Historically the total body of law has been made from acts of parliament and common law, custom and legal precedent. To arrive at a situation where all laws are fully documented as acts of the United Kingdom or devolved parliament an evolutionary process is required.

Each legal case brought by the judiciary must identify whether the case is brought under the laws of the United Kingdom or the laws of England, Scotland,Wales or Northern Ireland. The specific act is to be specified. If the legal case is brought under any other common law, precedent or custom then this is reported by the judicial branch to the legislative branch and the gap in the law is to be filled with new legislation so that an act of parliament or devolved government covers this case.

The government itself is bound by the law and legal cases against the government may be brought to the national judiciary. Depending on the nation in which the legal case is brought the appeal process goes through the courts of that nation up to the supreme court of that nation. This is the supreme court of England, the supreme court of Scotland, the supreme court of Wales or the supreme court of Northern Ireland. The supreme court of England has no jurisdiction over the supreme courts of the other nations.

If the action of the government applies to more than one nation or throughout the United Kingdom then the judicial review will be conducted by the house of lords.

**Article 4: Relations between England, Scotland, Wales and Northern Ireland**

The nations of England, Scotland, Wales and Northern Ireland form the country named the United Kingdom with devolved government in Scotland, Wales and Northern Ireland.

The nations of Scotland, Wales and Northern Ireland individually may decide by referendum for the nation to become an independent country. Depending on the decision of the devolved government, a referendum may be taken every ten years starting in 2100 to decide on national independence by a simple majority of the people of the nation.

For a devolved nation to seek independence they must have prepared a written constitution which will take effect as soon as the nation secedes from the United Kingdom and becomes an independent country. Within that country, the United Kingdom constitution will no longer apply but be replaced by the constitution of the new country.

The devolved nation will need to establish their own central bank to hold the accounts of the national government and to maintain financial discipline within the banks. A decision is needed on the choice of currency which might be the UK pound or the Euro or both. The UK pound is administered and maintained by the Bank of England.

The responsibility for nuclear weapons rests with the executive branch of the United Kingdom government. After independence a national government ceases its share in the responsibility for nuclear weapons and all nuclear weapon systems have to be removed from the national territory of the newly independent country prior to the independence referendum.

After independence an independent nation such as Scotland, Wales or Northern Ireland will cease to send MPs to the United Kingdom parliament and will not participate directly in the formation of United Kingdom law.

If during the devolution process, Scotland and Wales devolve into independent countries then it leaves Northern Ireland with a unique problem. Some of the people of Northern Ireland wish to remain a part of the United Kingdom while some of the people of Northern Ireland wish for a united Ireland.

The proposed solution is that Northern Ireland become an independent country, not part of a United Kingdom and not part of a united Ireland. Therefore as part of the devolution process from the United Kingdom, we need to protect the citizens of Northern Ireland from a unification with Southern Ireland which would be unwelcome by a substantial proportion of the population.

The Northern Ireland constitution constructed prior to devolution from the United Kingdom will state that it requires a four fifths majority vote in favour of Irish Unification with a turnout of at least four fifths of the Northern Ireland electorate. This constitutional arrangement has to be accepted by all political parties in Northern Ireland as a condition of holding a referendum on the independence of Northern Ireland from the United Kingdom. It is hoped that those who wish for a United Ireland will accept the final result of Northern Ireland and Southern Ireland as two independent countries.

## Article 5: Amendment process

Constitutional amendments may be originated by the government or suggested to the government by the people. After debate in parliament such proposed amendments will follow the process of legislation and if approved by the head of state must be put to a referendum of the people for a final decision.

It is of paramount importance that it is not possible for a dictator or autocratic government to seize power against the will of the people and extend their term of office.

## Article 6: National sovereignty

The sovereignty of England Scotland Wales and Northern Ireland is to be protected. The country is bound by international law but not subject to the laws of other individual countries. While international law binds the United Kingdom it cannot undermine fundamental principles of constitutional law and human rights.

It is a basic constitutional right for citizens of the United Kingdom to be tried by the courts of the United Kingdom. This constitutional right overrides the provisions of international extradition agreements with other countries.

The United Kingdom is no longer a member of the European Union and is not subject to the jurisdiction of the European courts.

To maintain sovereignty, United Kingdom law must take precedence over the laws and treaties of other countries outside the United Kingdom. As part of this constitutional change the United Kingdom must withdraw from the European Convention on Human Rights and create a United Kingdom convention on human rights. This will become part of United Kingdom law and be administered by the courts in England, Scotland, Wales and Northern Ireland.

The asylum system has long been abused by people traffickers to take advantage of people who are genuine economic migrants. The control of immigration is an important responsibility of government and the constitutional requirement to manage immigration overrides international law on asylum. Illegal migration is to be prevented. Legal migration is to be managed.

It is for the global economic system to resolve the issues in the country of origin that makes the people wish to leave.

## Article 7: Ratification process

This constitution is to be developed through debate and amendment prior to its first ratification. Once passed by the House of Commons, the House of Lords and signed by the Head of State it will be put to a referendum of the people. The government of the day may chose to adopt into law specific parts of this constitution which resolve a current problem without the need to adopt the entire constitutional change. This gradual process of evolution towards this constitution may be the most effective way forward.

## AMENDMENTS

### First Ammendment - Freedom Parliament

A freedom parliament is a parliament of independent MPs. It is so called because the party system is abolished and the party whips are abolished so that MPs are free to vote without party constraint.

Where political parties fight a general election there is a huge news media involvement and the whole election process is based on a celebrity culture to select a great leader. It is like a sports battle between two great teams with winners and losers and huge expenditure required to win the hearts and minds of the electorate.

By contrast under a freedom parliamentary election there are no political parties and each MP is elected by their constituents on the basis of their judgement of the candidate on the basis of honesty, trust and mutual respect and the policies that he would follow in government.

Under the party system the selection of candidates by each political party was a huge disincentive for people to enter politics. Firstly you had to pass the party selection process. The Labour Party would choose candidates who were trade unionists and ready to engage in the class struggle. The Conservative party would choose candidates who would favour big business and have policies in line with the wealthy people who fund the conservative party.

By contrast, ordinary people can stand as independents with very few restrictions. The prospect of serving in a freedom parliament where the culture is one of cooperation would encourage people with a genuine desire to improve things to come forward and not be daunted by what they saw in the past on television in the House of Commons.

Once the election is complete there would then be 650 MPs in parliament ready to select their leader. Any MP wishing to be elected prime minister by the parliament would identify themselves and state five key priorities that they would follow as leader.

MPs would vote on their choice of leader and the top five candidates would go through to the next round of voting. From the next round the top three candidates would be selected. Finally a third round of voting would select the prime minister. The prime minister would lead the government and set the agenda for government of the country with the main focus on domestic issues. With an end to geopolitics there is no sense in which a country needs a great leader to act on the world stage. What is needed is a person who will act with honesty, trust and mutual respect to resolve the current problems facing the country.

Any MP wishing to stand for a post in cabinet would make a choice of a maximum of three possible ministerial appointments. The cabinet positions would be filled in order of seniority starting with Chancellor of the Exchequer, Home Secretary, Foreign Secretary, Defence, Health, Environment food and rural affairs, Culture media and sport, Justice, Education, Equality of opportunity, Scotland, Wales, Northern Ireland and any other positions defined by the prime minister. One working day would be allocated for the selection of the candidate for each post. Thus the formation of a cabinet could take 15 working days or 3 weeks or more.

To elect the Chancellor of the Exchequer, all MPs wishing to fulfill the role would identify three key points for the economy and the plans of each candidate would be circulated to all MPs and the treasury. Each MP would have one vote and the three top civil servants in the treasury would have one vote each. The votes would be cast and the results of the voting including the names of the voters for each candidate would be passed to the prime minister. The prime minister would then select his chancellor of the exchequer from these election results, not necessarily having to choose the candidate with the most votes.

The process moves on to the Home Secretary and the three most senior civil servants in the Home Office would have a vote. Once the entire cabinet has been selected, there would be a vote of confidence in this government by all 650 MPs. If the prime minister loses this vote of confidence he would resign as prime minister and a new selection process would start looking for another prime ministerial candidate. A prime minister who loses a vote of confidence is not allowed to stand for the post of prime minister for one year from the date of the vote of no confidence.

If at any point during the parliament the speaker of the House of Commons receives letters from one hundred or more of the MPs expressing no confidence in the government then a vote of no confidence is taken in the House of Commons. If the government loses this vote, the selection process described above takes place to find a new prime minister and cabinet. If the government has been in office for more than four years of its five year term when the vote of no confidence is passed then a general election would be held.

The parliamentary programme would be decided by the cabinet and presented by the prime minister, not the head of state. Once parliament has decided on the new prime minister, this would be confirmed in a meeting with the head of state who would sign the appointment. The head of state may decide to decline the appointment of this prime minister if there is a good constitutional reason to do so. The head of state may apply a veto in this way only once following an election. Once all appointments are completed the government term is for a maximum of five years.

# 7 OPEN WORLD BOOK SERIES

**Open World book 1: The Evolution of the Universe.**

Presents a summary of the evolution of the universe which is finite with a space boundary. Galaxy formation takes place in individual galaxy formation events with energy for matter formation coming from expanding curved space. Galaxy formation started close to the centre of the universe at a time around 126 billion years ago and the position of subsequent galaxy formation moved away from the centre.

**Open World book 2: The nature of matter.**

Light travels as a wave in the medium of space. Matter particles such as the neutron proton and electron are looped waves in the medium of space. Starting from this wave oriented view the results of quantum theory and particle physics are explained.

**Open World book 3: The Conscious Brain**

Consciousness is defined as the subjective experience that we have from the operation of our brain. From this definition the importance of "Focus of Attention" is highlighted and a neuron network cause is described.

**Open World book 4: The Global Economic System**

An enhancement to the Global Economic System is proposed which is aimed at easing deprivation. It also provides incentives towards peaceful coexistence between nations of the world.

**Open World book 5: Openness**

The importance of guiding principles is identified. "I belong to a world in which all may live in peace following the principles of honesty trust and mutual respect. Honesty without fear; Trust filled with hope; and mutual respect for every individual person"

# ABOUT THE AUTHOR

I was born in the UK in 1946 and educated at Forest School and Cambridge University (St Catharine's College) where I read mathematics between 1964 and 1967.

I worked for the Marconi company for two years completing the graduate training program and then I worked on real time programming on the Myriad computer.

In 1969 I joined Northern Electric in Toronto Canada working on the real time programming of the No1 ESS telephone exchange. I joined Bell Northern Research in Ottawa in 1971 soon after its formation from Northern Electric and Bell Canada to work on the SL-1 digital telephone exchange where I led the software development for that product.

Returning to the UK in 1977, I worked for Nortel providing technical support for sales in Europe and the Middle East. I worked for three years in the city of London for Kleinwort Benson in the department responsible for providing telephone and data communications to the group.

I have always taken a keen interest in theoretical physics and cosmology and I have made use of published research on the internet, particularly from NASA (NED) and Wikipedia.

The papers on Academia have been published since retirement and I have obtained useful information from books and YouTube videos which describe the unexplained issues of physics and cosmology.

I am now working on Open World which seeks to answer some fundamental questions: How did the universe evolve? What is the fundamental nature of matter? How does the brain work? How should society organise economically? What are the fundamental ethical principles? How can we achieve personal, national and international peace?